MW01166624

Beyond Academics

Preparation for College and
for Life

Lee Binz,
The HomeScholar

First Printing, 2017

Printed in the United States of America
Cover Design by Robin Montoya
Edited by Kimberly Charron

ISBN: 1547250704
ISBN-13: 978-1547250707

Beyond Academics

Preparation for College and for Life

What are Coffee Break Books?

Beyond Academics is part of The HomeScholar's Coffee Break Book series.

Designed especially for parents who don't want to spend hours and hours reading a 400-page book on homeschooling high school, each book combines Lee's practical and friendly approach with detailed, but easy-to-digest information, perfect to read over a cup of coffee at your favorite coffee shop!

Never overwhelming, always accessible and manageable, each book in the series will give parents the tools they need to tackle the tasks of homeschooling high school, one warm sip at a time.

Everything about these Coffee Break Books is designed to suggest simplicity, ease and comfort — from the size (fits in a purse), to the font and paragraph length (easy on the eyes), to the price (the same as a Starbucks Venti Triple Caramel Macchiato). Unlike a fancy coffee drink, however, these books are guilt-free pleasures you will want to enjoy again and again!

Table of Contents

Introduction

Preparing for Adulthood

Homeschooling is not only about academics. Preparing your child for adulthood goes way beyond learning English, math, and science!

In this book, we will look at three overlapping areas that are important for success in both college and life: college prep activities to include on a transcript, skills for independent learning that all adults require, and health and safety issues that will prepare kids for a happy and healthy adulthood.

Colleges are interested in students who are well-rounded, students with life skills as well as academic skills. What are the skills that make your student attractive to colleges, and what activities will help your student develop those skills?

Children will eventually grow up and leave home (remember, this *is* your goal). They will need to understand adult responsibilities in order to succeed. How can you prepare your child to live independently?

You want your children to grow up to be happy, healthy, and firm in their faith. How can you know which health and safety issues to address in high school, so they can thrive? How can you equip them to thrive in the new environments of college and life, and maintain strong, healthy relationships with their family members?

The things you teach your children now are so important! Let's look at them together!

College Prep Activities

College prep activities are important, because colleges want to see well-rounded students ... students with more than academics, and interests beyond books. Your college prep activities can demonstrate your child's uniqueness.

Colleges look at a wide variety of activities, but also at activities a student has done over a long duration, such as three years or more. Colleges are attracted to students who show interest in meaningful activities over time.

Life Skills for Independence

Life skills are those skills necessary for people to function as adults. Again, independence is the goal. Whether your student goes to college or not, they will eventually live independently. You want them to thrive and not just survive, so teach them these life skills.

Health and Safety

I worked as a nurse at a hospital, so our family talked a lot about the different kinds of health. There's physical health, but there's also emotional health and spiritual health. You want your children to grow up, be happy, affirmed in their faith, and equipped for adult challenges. Talking about each area is important to your student's overall growth and maturity.

Chapter 1

College Prep Activities

Colleges want to see interesting students. Who can blame them? Wouldn't you feel the same way if you were faced with reviewing hundreds of applicants each year? Homeschoolers have the advantage because you have the time required for your students to become "interesting" in high school. It may start with a casual interest in middle school that blooms into a full-blown passion in high school. When this happens, it is a beautiful thing, and something you can use to your advantage in the college admission game.

These activities and learning experiences can (and should) be put on the transcript. My son, Kevin, played chess. It was an activity he engaged in for all four years of high school, and we put it on his transcript. During his first year, he studied chess, and we called it "Critical Thinking." In his second year he studied chess and taught it at local co-ops, so we called it "Public Speaking." In his third year, he taught chess and was paid for it, so we called it "Occupational Education," and put it on the transcript.

Usually these activities can be listed on the transcript, but they are easily forgotten. It's helpful to keep all activities on a list so you don't forget any.

Parents sometimes ask me how to get kids involved in an activity they are passionate about. The way we did it was to homeschool four days a week in high school, and then work on primarily interest-led schooling for one day a week.

There was still academic work our sons had to do on that fifth day, before they engaged in interest-led learning, such as math and foreign language. But beyond this, most of their subjects were completed in four days a week. They did the bare minimum of math and foreign language on the fifth day, and then the rest of the day was set aside for activities they wanted to do.

This fifth day was when our son, Kevin, played chess, taught chess, and studied chess. He even learned some Russian history later, mostly because of chess. It's also when our younger son, Alex, learned about the history of economics, and played piano. I encouraged my children to have passions. By allowing them to do school primarily four days a week, they were able to pursue their other interests.

Chapter 2

Leadership, Community Service, and Work

Leadership is something most colleges look for in an applicant. One way to foster leadership is to encourage kids to look at what they love doing and then try to teach what they love. Some kids will become involved in a group and some will become a leader in the group, such as Youth in Government or 4-H. There are many ways to be a group leader.

Students can work with their interests and abilities or can train or lead others at work if they're working at a job. If your student can find a mentor, that person can lead them and help them improve their own leadership skills.

Leadership is also something you can learn by reading about it. Read about leadership and about examples of good leaders, to become knowledgeable and skillful; then your child can act on that wisdom as they lead others. Leadership can be a subject you teach in your homeschool. Your class in "Leadership Studies" can include reading leadership books for teens.

Here's a list of my favorite leadership books for teens that we have read or used. Check them out to see if they are a good fit for your family.

- *Do Hard Things: A Teenage Rebellion Against Low Expectations* by Alex Harris, Brett Harris

- *The 7 Habits of Highly Effective Teens: The Ultimate Teenage Success Guide* by Sean Covey

- *Jesus Freaks: Stories of Those Who Stood for Jesus, the Ultimate Jesus*

Freaks by D. C. Talk and The Voice of the Martyrs

- *Rich Dad Poor Dad for Teens: The Secrets about Money--That You Don't Learn in School!* by Robert T. Kiyosaki

- *How to Win Friends & Influence People* by Dale Carnegie

- *Developing the Leader Within You* by John C. Maxwell

- These are some leadership books for teens suggested by my friends. I've heard some great reports about these books!

- *Love Works: Seven Timeless Principles for Effective Leaders* by Joel Manby

- *Created for Work: Practical Insights for Young Men* by Bob Schultz

- *Boyhood and Beyond: Practical Wisdom for Becoming a Man* by Bob Schultz

- *Real Citizenship: Practical Steps for Making an Impact on Your Culture* by Tim G. Echols

- *Being a Girl Who Leads: Becoming a Leader by Following Christ* by Shannon Kubiak Primicerio

- *One Girl Can Change the World* by Claudia Mitchell, and Kim Goad

- *The Gift in You: Discovering New Life Through Gifts Hidden in Your Mind* by Caroline Leaf Ph.D

- *The Slight Edge: Turning Simple Disciplines into Massive Success and Happiness* by Jeff Olson and John David Mann

Leadership was on the transcript for each of my children, but it wasn't something they particularly excelled in. Kevin taught chess, so we put chess coaching as his leadership activity, but they weren't involved in many groups, or as team captain or president of a club. Alex had the opportunity to teach one art class for a couple of months and we put it on his transcript, but leadership wasn't something I was good at fostering; it was merely something I attempted to cover!

Community Service

Community service is another big deal colleges want to see. There are even many schools that require volunteerism. I have a problem with mandatory work; it seems like an oxymoron, since you can't call it "mandatory" and "volunteer" at the same time. However, community service means your children are working without compensation for a charitable organization.

This requirement for community service goes beyond the standard academic requirements. Of course, your goal is for your student to serve with love, and hopefully for the rest of their life. For college admission, if your student counts their volunteer hours, you can record this on their college applications.

Many times, college applications will ask you to record the years your student served, which months, and how many hours they volunteered. Keep a resume of these activities, and include volunteerism separate from employment or regular school activities they participated in.

I'm the first one to admit that I failed in this area. My children worked a lot, and Kevin didn't have much time to spend in community service. Kevin taught a handful of chess classes early on in high school for no pay. Alex played the piano several times a year at church. So, technically we checked off the volunteer box, but I did not effectively cover community service, and wish we had done better.

There are more volunteer opportunities for your teens than you can imagine, but I have included a list in Appendix 1 to get you started. Whatever your teen is interested in, seek opportunities for them to serve others in that area. Not only do these activities improve their college admission applications, but they are foundational to help teens learn to think of others as well as themselves, an attribute you want them to learn along with laundry and budgeting!

Employment

Employment is another area colleges look at. It's not normal for children to be employed in high school, so when colleges see that hard work, they take note. Employment means working for financial compensation, and it can demonstrate diligence and a good work ethic. They call it work because it's not easy; it's hard and it demonstrates some stick-to-itiveness.

Chapter 3

Passion: The Secret Sauce

Passion is something colleges often talk about in their admission materials. Homeschoolers call it delight directed learning, but whatever you call it, it's important to spend some time developing it in your students.

People often ask me how to develop passion; I believe it comes from free time. Of course, the problem is that free time can be confused with couch-potato time, but it's *not* the same thing. Free time doesn't mean your student is free to play on the Xbox for 12 hours a day. Free time is when your children are bored (and unplugged). It's the time when they entertain themselves with delight directed learning.

Passion Requires Margin

Passion also requires margin. When you pick up a book, what makes the book easy to read is the large margin with space between the lines, so your eyes can easily follow the text. In your homeschool and your life, what makes a life easy to live is margin, a nice white space that is not filled with anything around your day. You might schedule your day, of course, but it's important to have a certain number of hours you aren't engaged or scheduled, for some free time.

This is important for teenagers, too. They need to have margin, so they can pursue what they are interested in, and not be scheduled and regimented all the time. Many of my friends feel strongly about scheduling every moment of every day for their children. As parents, you're trying to raise children who will grow up into adults, and adults need to learn to schedule their own time. It's good for them to know that school is their priority, but also be able to manage their own free time. How can they do this unless they have free time?

The Boundaries of Passion

Again, having free time doesn't mean there are no limits or boundaries. It's important to limit technology for your child to pursue their passion. Some kids are interested in coding or writing on the computer, but it's still important to limit games while allowing them to spend time coding. In general, limit technology, and allow them the time to experiment with activities.

When I was in high school, my passionate interest was health care. I knew I wanted to be a nurse, and I worked three days a week as a candy striper. Give your child the time and space to figure out their passion. It's important, both for their college prospects and for their own mental health and well-being.

Passion in Athletic Activities

Often, colleges look for specific athletic activities, but most don't have any requirements for admission. Many athletic activities can be done at home, independent of any school or club participation. Some homeschoolers want to be involved in school athletics, and that's fine, but you don't need to be involved in school to include athletic activities. My kids were involved in summer swim league, played soccer in the fall, and baseball in the spring for the first two years of high school, but got rather busy after that!

Some institutions, such as military and police academies, want to see proof of physical fitness, in the same way other colleges might want to see proof of academic achievement in the form of homeschool grades. Athletic activities can help provide this proof. Running track means running a 5K or 10K, but you don't have to be involved in a school. Of course, students may participate in community basketball, soccer, lacrosse, swim team, gymnastics, martial arts, or baseball camps. The options are limitless.

Passion in Non-Athletic Activities

Colleges also look for non-athletic activities, such as your church group, Junior Achievement, Boy Scouts and Girl Scouts, Boys and Girls State, or music. Students can get involved in a local band, orchestra, or theater, performing in local productions. Speech and debate teams are popular right now.

In my homeschool, there were quite a few activities my sons could have been involved in but weren't. We did participate in YMCA Youth in Government one year, but not in any other organizations.

If your child is interested in the Air Force, you might try to get involved with Civil Air Patrol. There are also the Army Cadet Corps and the Sea Cadets with the Navy, as well as the Young Marines. In some areas of the country, you can locate a Junior ROTC organization. Of course, in every area of the country you can find Scouts, and work toward becoming an Eagle Scout or equivalent. For those interested in the military, these are great activities that academies highly value on transcripts.

Chapter 4

The Teen with Multiple Interests

Let's suppose your child is the teen with multiple interests — *filled* with activities they *love* doing. Suppose your teen seems interested in *everything* and is engaged in learning a wide variety of subjects.

Sounds like a dream, doesn't it? I know that some of you are thinking, "I *wish!*" (If this is you, check out my How to Create an Extraordinary Activity List for Perfectly Ordinary Teens in Appendix 1). But the truth is that a child with multiple interests is as challenging as the unmotivated slug. Because, you know what? You can't do everything your child wants.

You can't fit in everything fun all in one year. There are four years to expose your child to a wide variety of fun activities so that when they become an adult, they can choose *which* is the most fun and determine possible career goals.

The first thing you need to realize is you can't do it all.

The second thing you need to realize is that your child is in charge of their interests, not you.

Keep the big picture in mind and it will seem less complicated. You need to provide the academics, that's true. However, it's possible to provide these academics (and provide them *well*), within a reasonable amount of time each day. It's also true that you can provide a high-quality high school education and work on a four-day schedule. So, as you are looking at your high school plan, think about which day might be the "light day," when you cover math, science, and foreign language, and then allow your child the rest of the day to pursue interest areas.

Here is how to break it down, so it will all happen, both the academics *and* the interests.

You are in charge of:

1. Teaching core classes in a way that gives maximum free time

2. Scooping up the natural learning your child is doing based on fun interests

3. Grouping those interests together into affinity groups called classes

4. Avoiding turning interests into school — instead, allow them to remain fun activities

Chapter 5

Independent Living

I didn't think much about independent living skills until my kids got older. They are important to teach, however, because you want your children to thrive and survive as an adult, whether they go to college or not.

Adults need certain skills to function on their own – they need to have some basic household tasks all figured out. They need to know about home economics, as well as auto-mechanics, even if it's as simple as knowing oil has to be changed or knowing where to go for the oil change. Even if you can't teach them how to change the oil, it's important they know what needs to be done!

Household maintenance is also important. Little things such as showing my kids how to change a light bulb didn't dawn on me until after my children moved out! Don't wait until your child has moved out to teach them the everyday life skills they need for success.

In addition to household tasks, students need to learn daily living skills. Even if they move into a college dorm room, they need to know how to do basic cooking, cleaning, laundry, shopping for what they need (and how to know what they need), and paying bills.

With regard to these daily living skills, I didn't do a good job of teaching my kids. I hardly ever had them cook while they were home, yet my married son Kevin does all the cooking for his family. I would never have guessed this in a million years, and I'm thankful for the few times a year I had him cook!

I did at least teach my sons how to clean the house. Every week all four of us got together and cleaned the house. Of course, I don't believe I ever saw them spontaneously clean, merely for fun. Fortunately, they know how to do the laundry, but shopping wasn't a skill I overtly taught, and I probably should have spent more time teaching them about paying bills.

Financial Management

Adults need to understand money, which means parents should talk to their kids about banking, balancing their bank accounts, paying bills, and paying their taxes. They need to learn how to make and stick to a budget as well.

In our homeschool, we talked with our children about having money to spend, money to share with charitable organizations, and money to save for a rainy day, as well as ultimately saving for retirement. When they were young, they had such a small income that banking was easy, so as they got older and their income increased, opportunities for learning expanded.

Work Skills

Equipping your children with work skills includes helping them look for a career and developing a healthy work ethic. Adults need to know how to learn, because when you're on the job, you learn new tasks. It's the skill of knowing how to learn that helps a person become a valuable employee.

Encourage your student to discover their passion, so they know what they want to do when they grow up, and what kinds of jobs they want to do. Perhaps your child is physical and needs to be outside working with their hands, or perhaps they're keenly interested in numbers. If you can help them discover their delight directed learning, then they will be able to pursue work that incorporates their delight.

Working can teach organizational skills. If your student has a job, they need to use an alarm clock; they have to know where and when they're going, how to get there, and all the organizational skills that go with a job.

For students with learning disabilities, this can be particularly challenging. One of my friends, who was homeschooled, had tremendous learning disabilities, but learned great adaptive skills because of his struggles. He went to work at Starbucks after high school and didn't have any trouble at all. He found out that he was a motivated hard worker, with a great work ethic and customer service skills. He succeeded in the work environment because of his adaptive skills. For kids who have learning challenges, work is an especially great opportunity to learn how to adapt to situations.

Community

Community involvement is important for maturity in young adults. They need to be involved in their communities, as well as organizations in their neighborhood. In addition to general community involvement, emergency preparedness is one of the ways students need to learn to take responsibility in their communities. Here in Seattle, we are prone to earthquakes, so our emergency preparedness usually boils down to being prepared for earthquakes and tsunamis. We keep two weeks' worth of food and water and learn how to help and work with neighbors in need.

In addition to community involvement, neighborhood participation, and emergency preparedness, teaching your children about voting is critically important. Teaching your children how to vote (not what to vote for, or which boxes to check) and the thinking process involved in voting is important, such as how to decide whether a person is the candidate for you, what to base your decision on, and how to make choices on issues.

These teenagers will be voting before you know it. Before you vote, I encourage you to sit down with your child, go over how to vote, and look at the voter's pamphlet together so they understand the issues. Save everything that comes in the mail on the election and talk with your child about how you make your decisions. Teach them to think before they vote.

Chapter 6

Health and Safety Preparation

Health and safety can be an uncomfortable topic to discuss with teenagers, but it's important to address. When you discuss health and safety with your students, make sure to talk about personal safety as well, which is important for children of both genders. Personal safety is a big deal. We think about it more for young women, because they often seem more vulnerable, but young men can also be affected in ways that can be devastating to their self-esteem. I think it is a good conversation to have with both boys and girls.

A lot of personal safety concerns situational awareness. Situational awareness has to do with being aware of what's going on around you, so you know what's happening. Even if you've trained your student not to text in the car, they need to keep their radio volume low enough, so they can hear what's going on around them. They need to keep their doors locked when they're in their car.

I recently saw a crazy video showing a guy walking while texting and running into a black bear in the middle of a city street. It was a wonderful graphic description of the importance of situational awareness.

Personal safety also involves assertiveness: when to stick up for yourself, when to make sure you use a loud voice, how to be assertive, and how to act as if you know what you're doing.

While it's important to educate your children and be aware of the risks, you also need to balance it out, and make sure you avoid fearfulness. The world is much the same everywhere you go. Sometimes things happen, and sometimes things don't, so avoid fearfulness but make sure your child is educated and aware.

Relationship and purity studies are also an important health topic for all teenagers. Look at books to decide which is the best fit for your family, and you can read and discuss issues about dating with your child. You might choose one book and include it in your health class. Or you might provide a significant reading list that becomes the cornerstone of your healthy relationships course. Here are my suggestions.

My Top Three Relationship Books

- For younger teens, *Passport2Purity* by Dennis and Barbara Rainey
- For older teens, age 14-19, *When God Writes Your Love Story: The Ultimate Guide to Guy/Girl Relationships* by Eric and Leslie Ludy
- For young adults, *Boundaries in Dating: How Healthy Choices Grow Healthy Relationships* by Dr. Henry Cloud and Dr. John Townsend

No book can be perfect for all families, and conversations can't be replaced with reading a book. I did some "crowd-sourcing" on Facebook to see what other families have used. In the context of conversations with your teens, you may find these books are a better fit for your family. Carefully read the book descriptions and the reviews. You want to find a book that matches your values but is challenging enough to make your teenager think.

Again, the relationship books below have been recommended by other homeschool families and I have not read them myself. Most of them are from a Biblical point of view. Carefully look at the descriptions to determine the best fit. Some of these books may be controversial within your friend group, and others may be too shocking or too staid.

You might like to provide multiple books on relationships for your child to read. My children are bibliophiles and that's what we did. You are trying to find a book (or books) that will be a challenging read, but not blow your child out of the water. You know your child best.

Relationship and Purity Studies Book List

- *And The Bride Wore White: Seven Secrets to Sexual Purity* by Dannah Gresh. For girls.

- *Before you meet Prince Charming: A Guide to Radiant Purity* by Sarah Mally

- *Changes: 7 Biblical Lessons to Make Sense of Puberty* by Luke (and Trisha) Gilkerson. Melissa says: "His books are wonderful."

- *Courtship and Dating: So What's the Difference?* by Dennis Gundersen of Grace and Truth books. Homeschooler Martha said, "The book is full of practical biblical counsel. Big fan of it."

- *Danger Signs of an Unhealthy Dating Relationship* by Lou Priolo. Dennis Gundersen, owner of Grace & Truth Books, recommends this book by a highly regarded Christian counselor.

- *Dateable: Are You? Are They?* by Justin Lookadoo and Hayley DiMarco

- *Dating with Integrity: Honoring Christ in Your Relationships with the Opposite Sex* by John Holzmann. This is sold with Sonlight Curriculum.

- *Every Young Man's Battle: Strategies for Victory in the Real World of Sexual Temptation* by Stephen Arterburn and Fred Stoeker

- *Every Young Woman's Battle: Guarding Your Mind, Heart, and Body in a Sex-Saturated World* by Shannon Ethridge and Stephen Arterburn

- *For Young Women Only: What You Need to Know About How Guys Think* by Shaunti Feldhahn and Lisa A. Rice

- *Gates & Fences: Straight Talk in a Crooked World* by Lori Wagner

- *God Is a Matchmaker: Seven Biblical Principles for Finding Your*

Mate by Derek and Ruth Prince. Angela said: "Excellent. However, the audience is for those ready for marriage. Derek Prince is a sound biblical teacher!"

- *I Gave Dating a Chance: A Biblical Perspective to Balance the Extremes* by Jeramy Clark. This book was recommended by Dr. Jay Wile of Berean Builders, author of the "Exploring Creation with..." series of high school textbooks.

- *I, Isaac, Take Thee, Rebekah: Moving from Romance to Lasting Love* by Ravi Zacharius. One mom wrote: "This one might be for older teens/young adults because it talks about marriage more than some of the others."

- *I Kissed Dating Goodbye and the sequel Boy Meets Girl: Say Hello to Courtship.* Author Joshua Harris has largely renounced these books; however, many homeschoolers still use them.

- *Let Me Be a Woman* by Elisabeth Elliot

- *Letters to My Daughters: A Dad's Thoughts on a Most Important Decision — Marriage* by Paul Friesen. One mom wrote: "Well-balanced approach to relationships from a Biblical view."

- *Love, Honor, and Virtue: Gaining or Regaining a Biblical Attitude Toward Sexuality* by Hal and Melanie Young of Raising Real Men. I personally know and trust Hal and Melanie for giving great advice!

- *The Mark of a Man: Following Christ's Example of Masculinity* by Elisabeth Elliot

- *Meet Mr. Smith: Revolutionize the Way You Think About Sex, Purity, and Romance* by Eric and Leslie Ludy

- *The Mingling of Souls: God's Design for Love, Marriage, Sex, and Redemption* by Matt Chandler. Megan, who is in college, wrote: "I highly recommend any dating/ relationship materials by Matt and Lauren Chandler. *The Mingling of Souls* has a part about attraction and dating and is also about marriage and I have used many of his resources for years. Very Christ-centered and helpful. I cannot suggest his materials enough."

- *More Than Just the Talk: Becoming Your Kids' Go-To Person About Sex* by Jonathan McKee. For parents.

- *Of Knights and Fair Maidens* by Jeff & Danielle Myers. This was recommended as a good, short book about courtship.

- *Passion and Purity: Learning to Bring to Bring Your Love Life Under Christ's Control* by Elizabeth Elliott (and Joshua Harris). This author is frequently recommended by homeschoolers I know and trust.

- *Passport2Purity* by Denis and Barbara Rainey. The book I used for my own children in middle school.

- *Relationships: The Key to Love, Sex, and Everything Else* by Dean Sherman. Recommended by Jill Bell, who also homeschooled boys.

- *The Sacred Search: What If It's Not about Who You Marry, But Why?* by Gary Thomas. Laura said: "This is an awesome book. I think every single person should read it, take notes, and read it again!"

- *Sacred Singleness: The Set-Apart Girl's Guide to Purpose and Fulfillment* by Leslie Ludy, the most frequently suggested author on this topic.

- *Sex180: The Next Revolution* by Chip Ingram and Tim Walker. Yuki says it's "excellent all-around teaching for guys and girls."

- *Sex Matters* by Jonathan McKee. Addresses the current youth culture and may not be appropriate for all families.

- *Sex, Dating and Relating* DVD by Marg Gungor. One mom wrote:

"This is a really good DVD series we used at home and at church."

- *Teaching True Love to a Sex-at-13 Generation* by Eric and Leslie Ludy

- *Ten Stupid Things Men Do to Mess Up Their Lives* by Dr. Laura Schlessinger

- *Ten Stupid Things Women Do to Mess Up Their Lives* by Dr. Laura Schlessinger

- *The Talks: A Parent's Guide to Critical Conversations about Sex, Dating, and Other Unmentionables* by Barrett Johnson

- *Wait for Me: Rediscovering the Joy of Purity in Romance* by Rebecca St. James

- *What Are You Waiting For? The One Thing No One Ever Tells You About Sex* by Dannah Gresh. Yuki wrote: "This is the 'why' behind 'wait' for girls."

I hope you enjoy this list and find something that makes it comfortable for you to talk with your kids.

Chapter 7

Physical, Mental, Emotional, and Spiritual Health

When your child lives in your home, you have quite a bit of control over their health, but you have less and less control as they grow up and move out.

Of course, your goal is to teach and equip them to take over the responsibility and control and become a healthy adult. I hate to say it, but there's nothing that speaks better to your child about health than your own example as a parent!

Physical Health

Physical health involves nutrition, fitness, exercise, and sleep. I did not teach my children much about nutrition, but I did model it well. In our home, we ate breakfast, lunch, and dinner together sitting down as a family of four almost every single day, from the time we started homeschooling until they graduated from high school. Statistics bear out how important these meals together can be for children's overall health, so try to work this into your home routine.

Our children were involved in sports, so they did learn about fitness and exercise. It never dawned on me to teach them, about the importance of sleep, however. I assumed that when people were tired, they would sleep. Of course, when they left for college, it didn't happen that way. Both of our boys (and their friends) had the same experience of going to college and deciding not to sleep, pulling all-nighters, and looking (and feeling) horrible the next day.

Make sure to teach your children the importance of sleep! In fact, I suggest that you assign your child a brief report on sleep, the value of sleep, and why sleep is important every year. Research supports its importance, too.

Mental and Emotional Health

The transition from high school into college and adult life is a time when students separate and become more independent from their parents. They're supposed to have some separation. They are supposed to grow up and become adults, but it seems as if parents are always surprised when it starts to happen!

One of the most recent factors to affect students' mental and emotional health is technology. In the current literature, there is a lot written about what a problem technology is for our children's generation. Studies have recently identified Internet addiction as a risk, in which children are addicted to their computers, much the same way a person might become addicted to gambling or pornography.

This doesn't mean technology is necessarily sin-based — I'm not talking about pornography. Often, this Internet addiction involves gaming, or more commonly for girls, social media. Considering this new research, it's important to assess your children and teach them boundaries in these areas, too.

In addition to Internet addiction, the wise parent will have conversations with their child about other things that can be addictive, such as alcohol, pornography, and drugs. While the typical homeschool family might not think too much about these issues (usually because your child isn't as exposed to such things), when your child enters the adult world, whether working or in college, they will encounter other adults who engage in these behaviors, so the need is still there to talk about them.

Having conversations at home is so much smoother and easier, no matter how awkward, than having conversations after your children are out of your house. Conversations about relationships — what is and isn't appropriate, what your family values are, and why — are also good to have early on, before your child will be in situations where they must apply these values.

I taught my children about relationships, but I didn't talk about the fact that other people would make other choices. When our sons grew up and went to college, some of their friends started living with their girlfriends, and that was a shock for our sons, who didn't quite know how to react.

Spiritual Health

Spiritual health includes talking with your child about their faith and your family's values. Although you can talk to them, such things are personal decisions, and your child must eventually make these beliefs and values their own as an adult. It's still your job as the parent to discuss faith with them, and what expressions of faith fit within your family values and which ones don't. Like any aspect of health, this too is a place where the example of your own personal life speaks more than any words you can ever speak to your child.

Chapter 8

Choosing a Major and Career Insights

We were sitting at the dining table, filling out college applications, and came to the part that said, "What is your major?" My son panicked.

It's rare for a teenager to know exactly what they want to do with their life. Few high school seniors can confidently say what their major will be. One step in the right direction is to do some career planning in your home.

Here are some resources that may help. Of course, don't expect a book or website to solve your child's problem, because learning your purpose in life happens over time, not in an instant.

Still, these resources can begin the process of thoughtful reflection.

Books

- *What Color is Your Parachute?* By Dick Bolles

- *Finding the Career that Fits You Workbook* by Larry Burkett. This is a Christian classic for career exploration

- *Do What You Are: Discover the Perfect Career for You Through the Secrets of Personality Type* by Tieger and Barron

Websites and Information about Career Exploration

- www.humanmetrics.com Personality tests, some free

- www.bls.gov/ooh "Occupational Outlook Handbook" (free)

- www.careerkey.org Personality related to occupations ($9.95)

- College and career planning on the

College Board site

- www.thecallonline.com "The Call Vocational and Life Purpose Guide" from Focus on the Family (Approximately $79)

- www.careerdirectonline.org Career Direct assessment from Crown Financial Ministries founded by Larry Burkett ($80)

- Finding Your Big Future by the College Board has a personality test for identifying your student's strengths, as well as college major and career suggestions.

Mostly, simply pick a major — anything! If your child is stuck, pick the hardest major they're interested in, not the easiest major. It's much easier to go from Engineering to Business than to go from Business to Engineering. The harder degrees often involve more difficult math and science. Meeting strict requirements will certainly meet requirements for the easier degrees. On the other hand, when your child chooses an easy major, the prerequisites are easy. Those easy science and easy math classes will *not* meet the requirements of a harder degree, so it could lengthen the amount of time spent in college.

Chapter 9

The HomeScholar
Five-Year Plan

In a recent sermon, my pastor said that kids grow up and become independent at a certain point, and they start making decisions on their own. Parents become limited in the amount of influence they have over their children. Your goal is to do the best possible job that you can while your children are in your home.

To evaluate whether you have succeeded in launching your child, you must think about what your definition of success is. Success has to be measurable, and the only way to measure your own success is by your own behavior. You can only define your success based on what you do as a parent, not based on whether your child turns out well, because you don't have control over any other human being except yourself.

What is not a definition of your success is the response of the child. It's up to them to take eighteen years' worth of advice and to keep it or not. Children do have free will, just like you and I do, and they can make adult choices.

When they make decisions, they make them on their own, uniquely, independently, and separate from you. You can't berate yourself for their adult decisions. Of course, neither can you claim responsibility for all their successes, either!

The HomeScholar Five-Year Plan

When my children were in college, I tried to maintain my sanity during their "capers" by keeping my five-year plan in mind. I kept in mind what I wanted life to be like five years from now. I wanted to have a loving family relationship, wanted my children to love God, to be happy and healthy, to be safe and sane, to be employed, and to live independently.

Keep your own five-year plan in mind, and it will help you maintain sanity in your home. If you focus on small things such as how messy their room is or how filthy their clothes are, it will probably lead to discord in your relationship. But if you focus on your five-year plan, it will help you calm down as you think through these different issues. Particularly after your children leave home, keep your plan in mind, and focus on your long-term goals.

When to Intervene

This does bring up the question, "When do you intervene?" This question typically comes up more often after children go to college, although it does come up from time to time when they're in high school. How do you know when to intervene, and when do you allow them to learn from their consequences?

You want them to learn, and you want them to face natural consequences, but only to a certain degree. My husband and I intervened when our children's behavior was life-threateningly stupid. It was threatening their life or their career, or they would face a lifetime of regret. Those are the times when you intervene, particularly when your children are college age. Keep in mind that some things kids post these days on social media can fall under this category. The internet is forever and so is every photo and status update they might post.

There's a huge transition time between high school and college. It's not as if your child suddenly grows up when they turn 18, and you allow them to suddenly face natural consequences. Their growth is more of a gradual change, so in the same way, you will gradually change when to intervene.

There aren't any hard and fast rules about it, either. I remember talking to one of my friends about facing natural consequences and intervening when it was life threateningly stupid. I used the example of helping them learn they're cold by not telling them all the time to remember their coat. But since my friend lives in the middle of Montana, and it's life threateningly stupid if a person doesn't wear their coat in the middle of winter, I guess that wouldn't count as a good time to teach this lesson!

Limitations

It is important to think about your own limitations as a parent. I think it's especially important to recognize that parenting is an extremely difficult job, and you can't do it all perfectly. Parenting is stressful, extremely tiring, and a lot of hard work. You can only do your best. I encourage you to do what you can and try your best.

I recently talked with my mother-in-law about the wonderful job she did raising her children; they all turned out reasonably well-adjusted, healthy, happy, and married for decades. A friend reflected that this success is because my mother-in-law genuinely loves her children. It's not because she had a college degree, and not because she trained her children well but because she genuinely loves her children. Remember that the love you have for your child will make a difference in their life. Your love for your child will help compensate for a multitude of shortcomings.

Appendix 1

How to Create an Extraordinary Activity List for Perfectly Ordinary Teens

The best part of homeschooling high school is engaging in fun and meaningful activities beyond academics. When not confined to public school desks for many hours each day, children have time to discover and explore their passions! High school activities are important, not only for the joy the experiences create, but also the impression they will leave with colleges and future employers. A list of high school activities becomes part of a comprehensive college application package and can be included on their resume for a job search. This will be a handy list to have!

There are two steps to making this perfect list with your perfectly normal children. First, you need to figure out some activities. Second, you need to include them on a list. Easy-peasy, right? Let me show you how and give you plenty of hints and tips. I'll even share a super-long list of ideas to help you brainstorm activities for your own, perhaps less-than-motivated teenager.

Create and Discover Activities

Not all children are naturally sociable and outgoing. Some are naturally quiet. If you have a child who seems to do "nothing", finding activities to put on a list can be a big challenge!

Sometimes the child isn't shy, but may have a family situation that makes building connections difficult. Some families, like our faithful military families, move frequently. Finding new friends and new activities in different locations every few years can be difficult. Yet, colleges will still want to see an activity list. Let's consider ways to find activities, because writing "nothing" on that application is not a good option!

What are Activities?

Activities can be extra-curricular, either before or after school work, or done during the summer. They can be athletics or team experiences. They can include hobbies or special interests. It might be employment, or volunteer work experiences or internship. It can include awards and honors received. It might be community involvement, or charitable work. It can be activities done only during the summer or year-round.

Your activity list should mention only things the student did after completing eighth grade, and before high school graduation.

Identify Something Fun

What does your child do for fun? If you think through each interest, you might find some great ideas for the activity list. For example, one of my children was constantly studying chess, and it helped me remember to put his chess experiences and awards on the list. Think about what they do for fun, and brainstorm everything you can think of that they do around their passion. You may strike it rich in activities there!

Family Evenings

What do you do in the evening as a family? What do you do on Monday night? Wednesday night? Sunday morning? Each of these family activities could be listed as an activity.

If you volunteer at a food bank, does your child go with you? Put that on the list. Do you attend church together, and your child goes to Sunday School or the weekly youth group? Put "Church Youth Group" on the list.

Double Check Classes

Sometimes your transcript will give you a clue to activities. If speech and debate is on the list — that's an activity, so include it on both the transcript and the activity list. Judo is a skill — put that on the activity list. Sometimes P.E. class involves an organized sport, or your fine arts class might involve an after-school theater group or club. I was involved in choir when I was in high school. I received a high school music credit for "Choir," and it was also included as an activity on my transcript.

Go over that transcript with a fine-toothed comb!

Memorable Moments

What has your child done that has made Grandma gasp? What did you put in your Christmas letter last year? Those memorable moments may include long-forgotten activities or awards. A shocking story that you told Grandma has not usually taken place in the quiet of your living room. Can that be a source of inspiration?

Student Teaching

One simple way to create your own activity is to have your child teach what they love. If they love Tae Kwon Do, they can ask their instructor for a job as a student teacher. An art-lover can volunteer to teach art to a group of friends. Your child can offer to teach classes at the local YMCA or community center. They don't have to be gifted at the subject; they only need to be willing.

Volunteer Activities

Volunteering together as a family is a wonderful way to develop an activity. Search your community for ways you can volunteer. Does your community have a food bank, clothing bank, or Meals on Wheels program? Does your church have a choir? Perhaps your child would like to sing in the choir or help lead worship vocally or with their musical instrument. Or perhaps they would like to take their musical instrument to a senior's center and play for them.

Have you gone on a mission trip as a family? Don't forget to add that to the list! Are you raising and/or training service dogs? Other places you can get involved in volunteering include: the United Way Youth Council, 4-H Teen Ambassador groups, Lions/Rotary/Kiwanis clubs, animal shelters, or your local library.

Each college or employer has a different way of asking about activities, so the more detail you include, the easier it will be to fill out forms. Employers might want this information in the form of a resume, and colleges may use the Common Application, or have their own forms to fill out. If you have the information you need, you will be ready for any requirement in the future. When you are working on college applications and they ask for information on activities, you will have everything you need at your fingertips. This can be such a relief during the "crunch time" of senior year.

Here are some websites for finding volunteer activities to do as a family.

The HomeScholar's Humungous List of Homeschool High School Activities from A-Z

When all else fails, and you can't think of any activities, check out this long list:

- 4-H
- Adopt a Highway
- After school tutoring programs
- Aide to the elderly, handicapped or chronically ill
- Animal rescue SPCA.org
- Animal shelters and rescue clinics
- Assisted living facilities
- AWANA
- Babysitting
- Backyard Day Camp
- Barn helper
- Beach clean-up
- Beach grass planting
- Boy Scouts
- Canned food drives
- Choir
- Church camps
- Church office or church service assistant

- Church youth group
- Civil Air Patrol
- Community center
- Community cleanup
- Congressional Award Program
- Costumed interpreter
- Crochet or knit for shelters
- Crossroads Kids Clubs
- Day camp counselor
- Daycare
- Debate
- DoSomething.org
- Elections
- Family Travel Network
- Fine arts
- Food pantries
- Foster kittens or puppies
- Gardening
- Girl Scouts
- Helping Hands
- Homeless ministry
- Hospital volunteer
- Jared Boxes
- Judo
- Junior ROTC
- Kiwanis Club
- Knit or crochet chemo caps

- Landscaping
- Library volunteer
- Lifeguard certification
- Lions Club
- Litter clean up
- Local community access cable station
- Make blankets for homeless shelters
- Martial arts
- Meals on Wheels
- MealCall.org
- Mission trip
- Museum volunteer
- Nursing homes
- Office assistant
- Operation Christmas Child
- Parks department
- Species surveys
- Perform at church
- Perform at hospitals
- Perform at retirement home
- Plant trees
- Political campaigns
- Post 4th of July cleanup
- Pregnancy crisis center
- Putting flags on graves
- Raise service dogs

- Reading buddy programs
- Red Cross
- Robotics Club
- Rotary Club
- Runs for a cause
- Salvation Army
- Save-A-Life
- School supply drive
- Science center volunteer
- Shelter volunteer
- Soup kitchens
- Speech and debate club
- Sports clubs or sports teams
- State parks
- Tae Kwon Do
- Teach art classes
- Teach chess
- Teach music lessons
- Teen Ambassador
- Teen Court
- Teen Pact
- Theater groups
- Therapeutic horseback riding program
- Tour guide
- Train service dogs
- Tutoring

- Umpiring sports
- United Way Youth Council
- United Way
- U.S. Naval Sea Cadet Corps
- Vacation Bible School
- Veteran's Home
- VolunteerMatch.org
- Walks for a cause
- Wild life rescue
- Worship team at church
- YMCA teen leaders program
- YMCA volunteer or activities
- Youth service clubs
- Zoo volunteer

(See: homehighschoolhelp.com/homeschool-activity-list for a printable list)

Remember that imitation is the sincerest form of flattery. Ask your friends! Look around at what other homeschoolers are doing for volunteer, leadership, and community service activities.

Appendix 2

The Perfect Launch Formula

You may be reading this book because you think I have all the answers and can bestow them on you. Well, you're half right; I do have all the answers, but I'm not telling! Just kidding! I'll tell you, but these truths, and how they should be applied, need to be discovered by each family alone.

I will give you the Perfect Launch Formula that experienced homeschool parents know all too well. From there, you will need to work out how it can help you succeed in your mission to raise happy and healthy adults!

Begin with the Perfect Launch Checklist:

1. Sound Educational Choices

Home education allows you to match your child's learning style with your family values. You can coordinate your child's temperament with your own organizational and teaching abilities. More important than your curriculum choice, is controlling your sense of urgency. It's so important to remember that education is not a race, and you don't get a prize for being the first to the finish line. You're not in a hurry, so you might as well enjoy the journey along the way.

2. Wholesome Home Life

A wholesome home life involves plenty of play, which means limiting the ubiquitous presence of technology. More pointedly, this means more face time with your child and less social media with your friends. A perfect launch requires a family to work together as a team, sharing the burden of household chores and educational responsibilities. A wholesome home life means avoiding swearing, name-calling, or belittling. It is encouraging to everyone, matching the goals and values within the home with mutual love and respect between all family members.

3. "Perfect" Parenting

The love you have for your child will ensure success, but being a perfect parent is impossible. Be patient, humble, forgiving, and extend grace. Confess your missteps, allowing others the freedom to confess as well. Be open to receiving advice and help from others.

Parenting is about time — children spell love, "T-I-M-E." Create enough margin in your home and work lives so every member of the family gets face time with each parent. Spend time individually, with one child at a time, in open dialog.

4. Model Character Development

Of course, you want to speak words of instruction to your child, but 90 per cent of character is learned by example. Parents must model consistency between their spoken values and behavior. If you want them to do their fair share, make sure you do yours. If you don't like what they watch on TV, what are you watching on TV?

Homeschool at home, so you have the time and opportunity to shape and mold your child's behavior during the day. You are raising an adult and encouraging them to become more civilized as they mature. Ignore this principle and you may end up with a feral teen. Be a role model your child can admire.

5. Faithful Religious Upbringing

Find the best fit for your child's moral and religious support. Find a good church, dive deep into the Bible, demonstrate and explain daily devotion to God. Find a network that will meet your children's needs. Your faith is already grounded while your child's faith is still forming, so prioritize their spiritual needs.

If you have an introverted child, find a youth group that will love them and not overwhelm them. If you have a budding intellectual, make sure they have exposure to mature and knowledgeable church mentors to get their questions answered thoroughly. Spiritual and moral maturity requires more than just teaching the Ten Commandments and the facts of life. Provide sound Biblical instruction while demonstrating a love for God in your own life.

Chronology of the Perfect Launch

The Bible shows us the chronological progression of a perfect launch.

"Train up a child in the way he should go … and when he is old, he will not depart from it." ~ Proverbs 22:6 (ellipses added)

Step 1. Parent's Role

We are called to train up our child.

Step 2. Child's Role

The child's role is in the ellipses … the implied pause in the middle. It is the indefinite time when the young adult must work out for themselves everything that occurs between "Step 1" and "Step 3."

Step 3. God's Role

God provides a promise that when they are old, your child will not depart from their training. Sadly, there are no hints about what "old" means — 18, 48, or 88 — we don't know. Experienced parents may know the heartbreak of waiting for their children to grow "old" and finally live in a way consistent with how they were raised. I hate to be the one to tell you this, but we aren't even guaranteed it will happen in our lifetime. Sad, I know ...

Perfect Launch SMART Goals

You must develop smart goals for your homeschool to truly measure your success. You see, children have free will. During "Step 2" of the chronology of their life, your child may take a circuitous route to responsibility and faith. All humans have free choice, even your child. Your child has the freedom to make stupid, bad, dangerous, and even sinful decisions, regardless of how much you love them, how much God loves them, or how much you pray.

No parent is immune to experiencing their child's sin nature. God, the perfect parent, still had to kick Adam and Eve out of the Garden for their sinfulness. The first human parents walked with God and had a depth of understanding of God we can only dream of, yet their child was a murderer. We can't measure our success by our children's actions or beliefs. Each parent must measure success only by their own behavior.

Create SMART goals. SMART is an acronym for "Specific, Measurable, Achievable, Realistic, and Timely." Specific goals might involve the classes you plan or tasks you want to accomplish this year. Measurable goals might include a daily devotion with your child or time spent playing with them each day. Achievable goals can only be ones you can reasonably expect to accomplish. "I will always be caught up with my ironing" and other pie-in-the-sky goals are not achievable. Daily hugs and words of encouragement are achievable.

Realistic goals adapt to your child's needs and abilities. Don't try to make your analytical, chess-loving child into a Charlotte Mason nature study loving child. Trust me on this one ... timely goals should be able to be completed soon (this week, this month or this year), not only within our lifetime or our children's lifetime. Your goals must be achievable by you, and under your control.

As much as you might wish, your children will not always be under your control. They will grow up and will make their own choices. Your success can be based only on your own behavior. Your adult child's behavior is their own responsibility.

I know this sounds foreign to newer parents who may enjoy a modicum of success controlling their little ones' behavior. When a two-year-old misbehaves, a parent can pick him up and remove him from the situation. When a 12-year-old misbehaves, a parent can send her to her room, or refuse transportation to fun events. But when a child is 18, or grown and gone, parents have no control over their behavior, beyond ordering the child to leave home.

While your child is homeschooling, set realistic goals. Accept your human limitation of fatigue but try your best. Like an athlete, leave it all on the playing field, and don't hold back any effort to shape and mold your child while you can.

Perfect Launch Guarantee

As you've probably guessed by now, there is no guarantee of a successful launch. If your firstborn is successful, it is not because you chose to make them successful. Awesome parents have children with free will, just as faulty parents do. While there are no guarantees of our children's ultimate success in their world, there is one thing parents can hold certain:

We are guaranteed God's loving kindness for us, and for our children.

God, as the perfect parent, allowed free will, even while knowing the consequences. The perfect parent had children who strayed. We can't change our children's launch into adulthood, for good or bad.

However, always remember, "The gifts and calling of God are irrevocable"

(Romans 11:29) and "He who began a good work in you will bring it to completion on the day of Christ Jesus." (Philippians 1:6). God is in charge of the ultimate outcome.

We can only control our part of the Perfect Launch Formula. We can give our children the tools and information they need to make healthy, wholesome choices for the rest of their lives. We can provide the wisdom and discernment they need to make choices we can't even imagine right now. Yet, we can't control their futures. Come to think of it, we can't even control our own futures!

Perfect Launch To-Do List

- Do your best.
- Pray hard.
- Love your child.

The Apostle Peter said it best:

"Above all, love each other deeply, because love covers a multitude of sins." ~ 1 Peter 4:8

Yes, love covers a multitude of sins and missteps along your homeschool path. It is your true Perfect Launch Formula.

Afterword

Who is Lee Binz and What Can She Do for Me?

Number one best-selling homeschool author, Lee Binz is The HomeScholar. Her mission is "helping parents homeschool high school." Lee and her husband, Matt, homeschooled their two boys, Kevin and Alex, from elementary through high school.

Upon graduation, both boys received four-year, full tuition scholarships from their first-choice university. This enables Lee to pursue her dream job — helping parents homeschool their children through high school.

On The HomeScholar website, you will find great products for creating homeschool transcripts and comprehensive records to help you amaze and impress colleges.

Find out why Andrew Pudewa, Founder of the Institute for Excellence in Writing says, "Lee Binz knows how to navigate this often confusing and frustrating labyrinth better than anyone."

You can find Lee online at:

HomeHighSchoolHelp.com

If this book has been helpful, could you please take a minute to write us a quick review on Amazon? Thank you!

Testimonials

The Best Resource on Homeschooling High School

"WOW!!!!!! I love the Comprehensive Record Solution. This resource contains it all!! This product is going to save many homeschool parents time, energy and money. It is by far the best resource I have seen on homeschooling high school for college preparation and admission. The written information is clear, concise and easy to use. The audio/video portions are easy to listen to and your chatty conversation-like style puts the overwhelmed homeschooler at ease. And you speak in the videos like a girlfriend who is going through all the same stuff with me! I feel myself saying, "YES!!! That was your experience too?!" It is soooo affirming. Your product is worth every penny and I can't wait to recommend this new resource to all my homeschooling friends. Great job and thank you so much for sharing your work, energy, time and expertise with the rest of us. You have been the best resource for my homeschool high school."

~ Sally in Washington

Very Professional and Detailed

"Sooo, I asked for feedback on my son's high school transcripts I submitted for early college. Since this is my first time homeschooling all the way through, I was pleased with these words: "You did an incredible job in putting everything together; the transcript, the course descriptions, the book list and report card. It is very professional and detailed. Typically more information is better than less. When I saw the records I thought it was a private school."

~ Valerie

For more information about my **Total Transcript Solution** and **Comprehensive Record Solution**, go to:

www.TotalTranscriptSolution.com
www.ComprehensiveRecordSolution.com

Lee Binz, The HomeScholar

Also From The HomeScholar...

- The HomeScholar Guide to College Admission and Scholarships: Homeschool Secrets to Getting Ready, Getting In and Getting Paid (Book and Kindle Book)

- Setting the Records Straight — How to Craft Homeschool Transcripts and Course Descriptions for College Admission and Scholarships (Book and Kindle Book)

- TechnoLogic: How to Set Logical Technology Boundaries and Stop the Zombie Apocalypse

- Finding the Faith to Homeschool High School

- Total Transcript Solution (Online Training, Tools and Templates)

- Comprehensive Record Solution (Online Training, Tools and Templates)

- High School Solution (Online Training, Tools, and Templates)

- College Launch Solution (Online Training, Tools, Templates, and Support)

- Gold Care Club (Comprehensive Online Support and Training)

- Silver Training Club (Online Training)

- Parent Training A la Carte (Online Training)

The HomeScholar Coffee Break Books Released or Coming Soon on Kindle and Paperback:

- Delight Directed Learning: Guiding Your Homeschooler Toward Passionate Learning

- Creating Transcripts for Your Unique Child: Help Your Homeschool Graduate Stand Out from the Crowd

- Beyond Academics: Preparation for College and for Life

- Planning High School Courses: Charting the Course Toward High School Graduation

- Graduate Your Homeschooler in Style: Make Your Homeschool Graduation Memorable

- Keys to High School Success: Get Your Homeschool High School Started Right!

- Getting the Most Out of Your Homeschool This Summer: Learning just for the Fun of it!

- Finding a College: A Homeschooler's Guide to Finding a Perfect Fit

- College Scholarships for High School Credit: Learn and Earn With This Two-for-One Strategy!

- College Admission Policies Demystified: Understanding Homeschool Requirements for Getting In

- A Higher Calling: Homeschooling High School for Harried Husbands (by Matt Binz, Mr. HomeScholar)

- Gifted Education Strategies for Every Child: Homeschool Secrets for Success

- College Application Essays: A Primer for Parents

- Creating Homeschool Balance: Find Harmony Between Type A and Type Zzz...

- Homeschooling the Holidays: Sanity Saving Strategies and Gift Giving Ideas

- Your Goals this Year: A Year by Year Guide to Homeschooling High School

- Making the Grades: A Grouch-Free Guide to Homeschool Grading

- High School Testing: Knowledge That Saves Money

- Getting the BIG Scholarships: Learn Expert Secrets for Winning College Cash!

- Easy English for Simple Homeschooling: How to Teach, Assess and Document High School English

- Scheduling — The Secret to Homeschool Sanity: Plan You Way Back to Mental Health

- Junior Year is the Key to High School Success: How to Unlock the Gate to Graduation and Beyond

- Upper Echelon Education: How to Gain Admission to Elite Universities

- How to Homeschool College: Save Time, Reduce Stress and Eliminate Debt

- Homeschool Curriculum That's Effective and Fun: Avoid the Crummy Curriculum Hall of Shame!

- Comprehensive Homeschool Records: Put Your Best Foot Forward to Win College Admission and Scholarships

- Options After High School: Steps to Success for College or Career

- How to Homeschool 9th and 10th Grade: Simple Steps for Starting Strong!

- Senior Year Step-by-Step: Simple Instructions for Busy Homeschool Parents

- How to Homeschool Independently: Do-it-Yourself Secrets to Rekindle the Love of Learning

- High School Math The Easy Way: Simple Strategies for Homeschool Parents in Over Their Heads

- Homeschooling Middle School with Powerful Purpose: How to Successfully Navigate 6th through 8th Grade

- Simple Science for Homeschooling High School: Because Teaching Science isn't Rocket Science!

- How to Be Your Child's Best College Coach: Strategies for Success Using Teens You'll Find Lying Around the House

- Teen Tips for College and Career Success: Learn Why 10 C's are Better Than All A's or APs

Would you like to be notified when we offer the next *Coffee Break Books* for FREE during our Kindle promotion days? If so, leave your name and email below and we will send you a reminder.

HomeHighSchoolHelp.com/
freekindlebook

Visit my Amazon Author Page!

amazon.com/author/leebinz